DESERT STYLE

DESERT STYLE

MARY WHITESIDES

PHOTOGRAPHY BY MATTHEW REIER

Gibbs Smith, Publisher
Salt Lake City

First Edition

07 06 05 04 03   5 4 3 2

Published by
Gibbs Smith, Publisher
P.O. Box 667
Layton, Utah 84041

Orders: (1–800) 748–5439
www.gibbs-smith.com

Edited by Jennifer Adams
Designed and produced by Ron Stucki
Printed and bound in Hong Kong

Library of Congress Cataloging-in-Publication Data

Whitesides, Mary.
Desert style / Mary Whitesides.-- 1st ed.
p. cm.
ISBN 1-58685-173-X
1. Architecture--Arid regions--Southwest, New. 2. Architecture,
Domestic--Southwest, New. 3. Architecture--Southwest, New--20th
century. 4. Interior decoration--Southwest, New. I. Title.
NA727 .W55 2003
720'.913--dc21
2002152816

CONTENTS

Acknowledgments

Desert Style is a beautiful book that I am proud to have published. I am always amazed at human creativity and love to explore the artful manifestations of the talented people I meet. The work of these interior designers, architects, and homeowners is imaginative, inspired, and visionary. It is sensitive to desert conditions and reflects an awareness of its fascinating history.

I would like to thank those people so responsive to my requests and those who helped me locate the wonderful homes contained in this book. Special thanks to interior designer Jo Taulbee for sharing her time and her work so openly. Thanks to interior designer Paul Faulk for his enthusiasm and generosity, and to Jill Jones and Sherry Thompson for their cooperation. To John Vrable, who made suggestions, and Brooks Pace, who spent hours helping me locate projects and allowing me to photograph homes in the Entrada community, I am grateful. Also, thanks to Kathy Bagley for her time in finding unusual homes.

Thanks to architect Hector Ramirez, designer/builder Bud Bracken, and Jim Dredge. A special thanks to Phyllis Woods of Tribal Links, Karen Kessler of Gallery 24, and Wes Baker of Borderlands Trading Company for their beautiful home furnishings. Thank you to Darcy Forman for connecting me to the right people. And an especial thanks to Gibbs Smith, Publisher for giving me this opportunity. And to Jessie, my daughter, thank you for your help.

Coven arches originated with the Moors as a means to save precious wood resources in the desert. The beautiful multiple arches in the entrance of this Santa Fe home are both dramatic and elegant.

Introduction

ELEMENTS OF DESERT STYLE

L iving with the harsh demands of climate and solitude, people have flourished in the desert for thousands of years. Historic building materials and methods, such as rammed earth and adobe, combined with modern style and contemporary conveniences have created a new look called desert style.

Desert style can incorporate any number of elements, from exterior design that creates homes that meld with the landscape, to interiors boasting modern art, old-world Tuscany design, or Spanish Colonial style. Open interior spaces, patios,

PHOTO BY MARY WHITESIDES

and well-placed windows are often incorporated in the design to create openness and to extend living space into the outdoors. Water, a precious commodity in the desert, can be used in fountains or reflecting pools whenever possible to create a sense of oasis in a dry environment.

By selecting certain building materials; incorporating specific colors, textures, and shapes; and aligning oneself with a philosophy of conservation, desert style can fit into most life-styles. Incorporating any or all of the following elements in your home will help create a desert-style dwelling.

ANCIENT MEETS MODERN

All of civilization took root in the desert. Paleo-Indians lived in permanent structures known as pit-houses dug in the ground; modern structures have learned from their insulating properties. Later, above-ground communities were built of stone masonry, such as Mesa Verde in Colorado. Modern stone masonry techniques and styles have found inspiration in numerous ways from such structures. The simplicity of ancient stone work translates easily into a multilevel home that suits contemporary needs. Other age-old methods for building, such as rammed earth, are once again popular.

PHOTO BY MARY WHITESIDES

Modern design and conveniences blend with ancient architecture and methods in desert style. An outdoor fire pit sits next to a Jacuzzi. A wall of rammed earth or Venetian plaster is flanked with stainless steel kitchen appliances. Furniture or ceilings incorporating vigas define a room that holds a modern entertainment center and big-screen TV.

BLENDING ARCHITECTURE WITH LANDSCAPE

On a remote landscape such as the desert, where the beauty is fragile and precious, the design of a home should meld with the existing topography: in other words, the architecture should blend with the landscape. For desert-style homes built in a dense urban neighborhood rather than in the desert landscape itself, the home can center more on the interior architecture, colors and textures, furniture and décor to achieve the right feel. Landscaping should incorporate vegetation that complements the home's natural setting and should be conservation-sensitive.

BUILDING MATERIALS

Desert-style homes are often built with organic materials such as rammed earth, adobe, or stone masonry. Aesthetically, these materials fit well into the landscape. They also pay tribute to the age-old civilizations of the desert. Leave-in-place concrete forms or similar systems for building thick stable walls are also an option. Such materials are easily obtained and have strong insulating properties. Homes built with these materials are ideal for desert conditions, as they regulate temperatures to keep homes cool in the summer and warm in the winter without huge outputs of energy for heating and cooling.

OUTDOOR LIVING SPACES

Desert homes should not compete with the sweeping landscapes on which they are sited. Instead, homes should blend into nature without trying to dominate it. By blurring the line between interior and exterior, you can incorporate outdoor living spaces into your home. Placing glass behind shelves or around a fireplace leaves open views of the landscape. Skylights, glass walls, sliding doors, and patios that continue flooring materials from inside to outside seamlessly connect the interior of the home to the outdoors. You can also take advantage of the solitude and openness

of desert living by leaving windows exposed to the outside without curtains or blinds. Many desert homes have balconies, decks, Jacuzzis, and patios to encourage outdoor living.

Colors such as umber, terra-cotta, brick red, and eggplant are complementary desert hues. The iron-rich soils of many southwestern deserts are responsible for the deep rich colors of the landscape as seen in this painting by fine artist Kim Whitesides. The free-form chair is a masterpiece of desert-dried tree limbs upholstered in a kilm woven in the Kalahari desert.

OPEN INTERIOR SPACES AND VAULTED CEILINGS

Two styles that suggest desert living are Old Spanish Colonial and Tuscany. These styles often call for implementing vaulted ceilings, coves, and arches into interior designs. The vaulted ceilings of old Spanish missions are dramatically embellished with ornate wood patterns. Intricately carved and painted ceilings are often viewed through rows of beams and carved corbels. This kind of ceiling, of course, requires a voluminous space. Sculptures and rustic furniture often work well in these kinds of settings.

PHOTO BY ERIKA BLUMENFELD

COLOR AND TEXTURE

Floors, walls, and ceilings set the tone for the home and are a central place for the expression of color and texture. Depending on your budget, you can use materials and finishes that run the gamut from techniques employed by the finest craftsmen and artisans to do-it-yourself methods.

When creating desert style, work with a selected color scheme. Choose colors that complement or contrast with the surroundings. Subtle tones such as buff, chamois, or buckskin complement desert colors. If you choose the old-world look, colors will be deep, rich, and contrasting. Umber, terra-cotta, brick red, eggplant, subtle oranges, and soft cream colors lend themselves to a warm casual setting. Southwestern colors include rich browns and reds, a spectrum of oranges, and subdued greens.

A concrete floor is a superb canvas for the ancient, contemporary, old-world, or updated southwestern desert style. Slate and limestone flooring in all colors is standard in many homes today, and the textures and colors are judicious choices for a desert look.

Various woods are also plausible choices to establish the mode for a contemporary desert style. For example, bleached oak and limestone synchronize handsomely as a neutral backdrop in a contemporary home. Soft colors can calm the living area in a way that widens the interaction between interiors and the outdoors. Various woods such as aspen, alder, and pine can be bleached and wax-finished to achieve flooring with a very clean look.

FURNITURE AND DÉCOR

The selection of furnishings and décor for a home is a simple way to implement a style. For desert-style homes, furnishings with quiet upholstery colors and medium-to-light wood tones are good choices. Lighter tones can be accented with stronger colors. When selecting furniture, look for pieces that evoke simple, clean elegance like that which comes from the desert itself—uncomplicated in its beauty.

PHOTO BY ERIKA BLUMENFELD

Plain pieces of furniture can be embellished. Carved motifs generally used as wall ornamentation can be applied to chests, boxes, armoires, drawers, and cabinets. An entire room can change in look and period when the right accessories are selected and arranged. Rusted metal has a broad application in desert style; incorporate it with lamps, boxes, racks, and shelves. Ornamental iron panels can be used above doors and on walls as accents. When searching for accents, look for pots, urns, and antique wooden bowls, then use them in surprising ways. A very large urn can serve as a receptacle for a guest bathroom sink. Pots placed in piled collections add dimension to a table. Wooden bowls used in the bathroom for towels and soaps organize in a delightful way.

INCORPORATING WATER

A rare commodity in the desert, water is precious and should be both highlighted and conserved in dry-climate residences. Many desert homes have the focus of a fountain or reflecting pool. The cooling sound of water makes the home feel like an oasis—a safe haven in a harsh climate.

PHOTO BY MARY WHITESIDES

Water conservation should always be considered, including the use of water-saving toilets, showers, and faucets. Look into Xeriscape gardening methods, which use native vegetation watered by drip irrigation. A careful study of water limitations should always be considered, including evaporation rates, and water features designed accordingly. Streams, waterfalls, and fountains can all operate on a pump-and-recycle system. Windows, doors, and rooflines should be oriented to maximize heating, cooling, and ventilation.

INCORPORATING ART

Art—whether paintings, sculpture, or crafts—can individualize and personalize a home like no other element. While exterior architecture sets the tone of a home and interiors enhance our standard of living, it is art that feeds the soul. Desert architecture and interiors make an earthy statement, tying in with nature. Nature can be complemented by art in many different ways.

PHOTO BY ERIKA BLUMENFELD

Selecting art is not difficult. The best selections with the most meaning are made from the heart. If an artist is good, his or her work will reach out and touch your senses and intuition. Select these kinds of pieces to grace your walls and shelves, your entrances, living rooms, and gardens. Take into consideration the space you wish to enhance, the colors that will be harmonious, and your own tastes and preferences. Desert style presents a radiant palette of inspiring elements. The desert itself is a clamorous influence, provoking the best work of many fine artists.

CONCLUSION

A home should be an artistic expression of your individual taste. Desert style, in its wide range of applications, can be a way to express your tastes. From a guest's first impression on being invited in, to a family's ability to relax in comfort, your desert home should be beautiful as well as functional. Live your philosophy, establish a sense of place, and express yourself. As you create your own expression of desert style, remember to love nature, honor history, and live with art.

ANCIENT MEETS MODERN

The ancients lived simply in the desert, using mud and rammed earth to build their shelters. Modern architecture has come full circle: the materials used to build this house are also of the earth—uncovered, unconcealed, and unpainted—a crosscut of the environmental milieu looking like a geologic study. Tamped one layer at a time, the structural walls of the home imitate the stratification of the surrounding soils. Earth from the excavation of the site was used, mixed with 3-percent concrete to act as a bonding agent. From a distance the house looks like a contemporary concrete structure. On closer inspection, the textured walls resemble an ancient Indian site, tactile and divinely organic.

The architect settled the house low on the rugged Tucson landscape, the inverse roofline a flopped version of the mountain behind it. The winged pitch of

The inverse roofline of this rammed-earth home is a flopped image of the mountain behind and directs rainwater away from the house.

Left – An uncluttered galley kitchen combines elegant maple cabinets with trendy stainless appliances and earthy concrete floors. The kitchen is open to the living room, allowing guests and chef to share culinary duties and conversation. Above – The L-shaped structure of the house frames a courtyard where nature is the caretaker. Below right – A tiny, thick bubble-glass window reflects striated light like a piece of installation art.

corrugated metal directs whatever rainfall that may occur out and away from the house and shades the house from afternoon heat.

Granddaddy saguaro cactus—human-like guardians—surround this carefully situated residence. Few to none of the cactus were destroyed during construction, fragile as they are. Most houses in the Tucson mountains leave landscaping to nature.

On the interior of the rammed earth home, the blending of modern and ancient again comes

into play. Some of the furnishings look corporate; others antique. Accents are ancient African and pre-Columbian. The architecture and furnishings mingle in a simple environment without the threat of clutter. Living in this house is like dwelling in a desert cave. The massive solid walls heat very slowly in summer, allowing the house to

This laundry room has a touch of elegance. It doubles as office space where glass collections are displayed and computers mingle with laundry soap. Well-placed windows assure a cool atmosphere and well-directed light.

Extensive roof-overhangs
and a closed terrace pro-
tect a glass bathroom from
the light and heat that
could otherwise be glaring
and harsh in this desert
climate. Mirrored walls, a
milk glass shower back-
drop, and sliding glass
doors invite the outdoors
in, reflecting nature around
the room.

PHOTO BY MARY WHITESIDES

remain comfortable without air conditioning. In winter the walls cool slowly.

The rooms are open, spacious, and clean. The waxed concrete floors tend to cool the atmosphere, which is most welcome in the dead heat of summer. The slanted plate-glass walls of the living room face the Tucson Valley with a panoramic view. The kitchen is wide open to the living room—its contemporary maple cabinets and stainless steel appliances another example of integrating modern elements into a home built using ancient materials and methods.

Other elements that reflect desert style are simplicity and the clean flow of space. No space is wasted in this Zen-like home; every inch has a function so that no

space sits empty or unused. Even the laundry room doubles as a home office. The bedrooms are without muss or fuss, leaving the idea of sleeping pristine. No headboards, rugs, or extra chairs grace the room. Only a stool made for African royalty sits in the corner, along with shaman figures. Simple black-and-white photos by Nancy Glazer grace the walls.

The bathroom is a testament to the privacy enjoyed by this desert resident. Sliding glass doors, flush from floor to ceiling, daringly expose the shower to the outdoors. The room collects a plentitude of natural light. For this homeowner, starting the day in simple surroundings sets the tone for the workday as would meditation.

African artifacts throughout the house are not without connection to the desert. The Dogon peoples are perhaps the oldest living culture of the North African deserts. Above – An African stool is used here as a work of art but in the African culture functions as a royal seat. Left – Three African icons stand vigil over the house as though guardians of time immemorial. Right – Outdoor living is welcome on hot arid afternoons and cool desert evenings. Roofed and sheltered by two walls and open on two sides, this outdoor room funnels a cool breeze summoned by a ceiling fan and cozies up with a fireplace after dark. A lone door from the Dogon culture leans detached from its origins but functions beautifully as a sculpture.

An outdoor living room, half-sheltered by two walls and a roof, is exposed to the elements on two open sides. A fireplace adds ceremony and gives the comforting feeling of a campfire in the outdoors. A daybed allows this outdoor space the option of becoming an extra bedroom. A single antique door from the desert Dogons of North Africa leans petrified in time against the earthen wall, one more reminder that ancient meets modern in the apex of desert style. The Paleo-Indians who lived on this land six thousand years ago would take comfort here.

Above - An ingenious metal sheath houses a utility meter from the harsh desert heat. Situated at eye level, the dials are easily read. Left – A rusted steel header above a doorway is not only structural but adds a visual element as well.

Corrugated metal roofing is a dramatic part of the architecture and also provides a sizable overhang that shelters walls and windows from the sun. In addition, the slant and grooves catch rainwater, directing it down and away from the house.

2 | BLENDING ARCHITECTURE
with Landscape

PHOTO BY MARY WHITESIDES

A porch of open vigas filters light in patterns on the face of the entrance to this southern Utah home.

This deep-colored adobe home spreads low and lean on the desert floor. It is a reflection of pueblo adobe style, which is now an American Southwest classic. As dynamic as the structure is, it is not easily seen by the neighbors. Strict building codes are mandated in Kayenta, Utah, where locals are sensitive to preserving the visual integrity of the area. Only 25 percent of an owner's property can be built on. The oversized lots keep the housing density down. With the exterior building height limited to thirteen feet, the two hundred homes cannot be seen from the highway one mile away. No two-story homes are allowed unless a hillside buffers the house. A few owners dig their homes into the ground in order to have higher ceilings and windows to take in the views. The earth tones of the adobe walls blend with the mountains and match the subtle variations of the soils behind them—some deeper in color, others lighter.

Strict lighting codes (including a clause on skylights) are in place so as not to impair the nighttime heavens. The owner of this adobe says, "We were even sensitive to the size of the windows around our dining area. In some ways we had to put up with the restrictions but we knew the whole community would be affected." These codes ensure the owners' enjoyment of their move from Florida to a home in a more austere atmosphere is protected. It is the beautiful colors, the landscape, the quiet, and the stars that keep them here.

Appointments in the homes of Scottsdale and Santa Fe—the wood on the ceilings, the plaster, and the special shapes and curves of the walls—are interpreted to a

Left – A sizable country kitchen adds to the eclectic nature of this adobe home. Distressed charcoal cabinets and deep rich wood floors contrast with the soft creme and tan colors of the tile and walls. A central island with chopping block doubles as ample work space for the chef and as a casual countertop for breakfast. An antique wagon wheel doubles as pot hanger/light fixture, while the skylight above the counter gives a sense of airiness and space. Right – *Vigas* on the living room ceiling are individually cut on the floor then assembled above to fit curves and angles. A graceful feminine wall curves around the *vigas* to the fireplace, softening the otherwise sharp angles of stone.

fine degree in this home. Over a period of five years, the owners acquired antique treasures found in the Southwest, which inspired certain design elements in the interiors. Scavenger hunts turned up special details such as old shutters and lighting fixtures with textures and shapes that could be incorporated in the design. The primitive doors and the big wheel hanging in the kitchen are from Santa Fe. The wagon wheel doubles as a light fixture/pot hanger. "One set of shutters that we hadn't a place for were considered awkward by the builder," the owner says. "He thought they would be too narrow to use as functional doors and ended up building them into the wall as a pass-through in the butler's pantry behind the kitchen."

Above – The *kiva* traditionally used by Native Americans for sacred ceremonies provided the architectural inspiration for the dining room. Used as a starting point for design, this circular space was the impetus for the entire house. All rooms radiate out from this center point. Right – An inordinately long shelf greets and draws a visitor into the house. Art and sculpture set an immediate tone of serenity and creativity.

The walls have a sheen that can only be achieved by polishing several times—a method called *diamond finish.* The detailing is precise and the work requires a trained artisan. Unlike the loose uneven strokes of Venetian plaster, this method leaves a smooth luster on the walls.

The home incorporates pueblo adobe style in interesting ways. In the dining room, the architect pays homage to the Native American ceremonial rooms called

Left – The natural earthen quality of adobe is paired with a timeworn wooden door. Once part of an old colonial home, a stand-alone arch now leads down a garden path. Right – A contrast in color and texture are achieved by a careful selection of materials. Slate flooring with its uneven surface and varied earth tones polarizes the smooth diamond finish plaster on the walls. The extraordinary elegance of marble shelving used on this display vignette juxtaposed next to a natural log column is unexpected, surprising and pleasing to the eye.

kivas. The plans for this room were developed early in the design process, driving the look of the surrounding spaces. On the floor plan it was difficult to comprehend the curves that hovered above the floor. The overhead walls didn't become apparent until construction began. The owners came to fully understand the concept once they visited Mesa Verde.

"I don't generally like round tables and had planned on a rectangular one for that space," the owner says, standing next to her very round table. However, eventually she began to embrace the concept of *kivas,* and the living room grew out of the circles and curves of that room.

The *vigas* in the living room are individually cut—one with an inside slant and the other with an outside slant—in a way that, when installed, hit a curve on both ends of an angle. They are cut on the ground to fit the ceiling; it is remarkable how well they fit.

The diverse furnishings reflect a number of life-style changes for the owners over the years, ranging from classic to mountain to desert. "We combined some of our traditional furnishings with what we thought went in a desert home," commented the owners. They started collecting artwork, with the architectural plans in hand for several years, and many of the sculptures and paintings were bought just for the home. "Certain places were built to fit the pieces we already had," they explained. Large niches on each side of the great room house two commanding bronze pieces—a chief's headdress and a cowboy with his lariat.

The mud-covered structures of the ancient American Indians, patrons of desert history, are one inspiration for modern desert style. With this home we see that pueblo adobe style endures.

Left – Slivers of light shine through a beveled glass door composing patterns in this hallway, which displays heirlooms singled out as meaningful statements of family. Collections such as this painting, grandmother's tea set, and a classic mahogany table are beautiful pieces to individualize a desert home. Right – This home is truly a celebration of nature, history, and art. The terra-cotta adobe looks to be an extension of the surrounding cliffs, the territorial porch reflects early Spanish Colonial architecture, and a bronze sculpture displays joy in its surroundings.

3 | BUILDING MATERIALS

I f you stumbled upon this stone house while looking for the ruins of the Anasazi Indians, you could be fooled into thinking you had found them. Even the Native American steppe pattern on the aged copper edging looks ancient. The stonework

Random quartzite walls and the copper fascia that edges the roofline of this home suggest an older time with a modern twist. The courtyard is a quiet oasis that beckons a soul to stop and contemplate. Koi swim in silent meditation and the sound of water tantalizes the senses.

Local quartzite imprinted with desert colors form pillars and walls inside and outside this house. Colorado limestone refines the space. A marriage of styles and elements always personalizes a home. In this case, Indonesian artifacts create a cohesive bond between the desert and the owner's homeland.

resembles the masonry of ancient Mesa Verde, although on closer inspection it is more refined. Angular shapes, both vertical and horizontal, also reflect Native American style. This home is a clear example of the influence that Native American structures in the Southwest have had on contemporary desert style.

The quarried stone used on the façade has a timeworn patina, adding to the ancient look of the home. Sunburnt umber tones, watermarks, lichen, and wind-worn ripples all contribute to the character of this natural quartzite. The primordial stone is genuine desert archeology.

Native Americans used courtyards as public gathering places; the Spanish used
them as breezeways to help cool spaces. Hidden behind low stone partitions, here
too are courtyards. Water is used in pools and fountains to bring a cooling effect to
this desert home. It also adds to the feng shui, as brightly colored koi fish swim
silently beneath lily pads.

From the road, the front of the house looks tucked in as a single story but
opens to a venerable multistoried arrangement in the back. The ancient stone from
the house façade is used on the interior walls. Large windows frame dramatic red

The architecture of this desert-style home pays strict attention to dramatic views of red cliffs. A duck pond meets the edge of an infinity pool like a mirage from film noir. Glass walls function as picture frames around the environment, but are technically situated in a northerly direction to avoid collecting heat.

cliffs. In the foreground, a view of an infinity pool meeting the edge of a duck pond looks to be a mirage.

Use of limestone in the entrance gives a refined look to the sunbaked surroundings of the desert. Brazilian cherry wood floors, beams, and staircases resonate with the deep vermilion colors outside. The steppe pattern defining the exterior roofline continues inside as a theme on doors, stair railings, and moldings, all milled by local craftsmen.

The house is situated with such dramatic views that interior designers from Denton House Interiors took a softer approach with the color scheme, choosing colors that blend with rather than rival the brilliant outdoors. They chose home furnishings in muted colors that are restful to the eye and do not compete with the raging reds of the vermilion cliffs. Sofas, chairs, and tables have classic lines. In this clean

A high ceiling latticed with beams hovers over a dignified room in which to conduct business. An antique carved panel from Bali accentuates this home office space, clean and precise in décor.

and simple setting, ornate antique accessories become the focal point. The owners of the house have strong ties to Indonesia and mix their love of Indonesia and the Native American desert masterfully. Such decorations as hand-carved statuettes, paneled screens, and a man-sized gong adorn the hallways, den, and master bedroom.

Left – Brazilian cherry wood floors express eloquence in the master suite. A touch of quartzite on the fireplace is the unifying component found throughout the house. Open, spacious rooms such as this extend the desert vista indoors. Spatial orientation and carefully placed windows assure maximum enjoyment of the environment. Right – Conveniently located behind this sweeping bar is a state-of-the-art wine cellar. The temperature is regulated perfectly to preserve aged wines. The alder wood countertop has been soaked and bent to a precise measurement capping the stone base. The copper railing, also masterfully curved, is placed a shoe length out from the bar.

The ground level of the house is geared around welcoming guests. The sweeping bar of stained cherry wood is a gathering place for a social drink and conversation. A pool table just steps away makes it easy to join in a game of billiards. The adjacent conversation room has the elegance of leather chairs and sofas, where one can recoup from a vigorous game. An immense stone fireplace with a wall-to-wall mahogany mantel is defined by a single brass gong.

Above – A steppe pattern theme from the copper fascia on the roof edge is a means to interweave outside details with inside. This stepped stair railing of solid cherry wood is artfully connected by copper wire, suggesting sun rays. Left – A massive mahogany beam serves as a mantel and defines the recreation room. It extends far beyond the confines of the firebox and theatrically provides a showcase for artifacts. Right – An infinity pool dramatically reflects this architectural masterpiece. Desert style at its finest under a night sky.

As millions of stars arrange themselves in the night sky, one can wander onto the patio for a private view of the light show that only the desert can provide. If guests are enchanted beyond thinking of retiring, a soak in the hot tub, brightened by a pit fire, may keep them up all night. And perhaps while looking through the open fire back at the house, a vision of Mesa Verde might inspire the imagination.

4 | OUTDOOR LIVING
Spaces

Indoor/outdoor living is one of the most pleasant ways to live in the desert. Architecture must be in scale with the native vegetation. Plants do not grow tall or lush, so careful use of opaque materials becomes important. Exteriors must be understated for minimal visual impact. If a neighbor looks out and sees another house, it should blend in with the surrounding topography.

Left – A wall of windows blurs the edges between indoor/outdoor living. On the far end of the room, these massive windows slide into wall pockets connecting patio and sitting area, dining room, and kitchen. Below – Architecture blends with topography.

A shelter for living outdoors in the desert best describes the Moenkopi House. The architect sculpted the structure around two gigantic stones as a living piece of

art. The impetus for the design radiated from the stones themselves, and the result is a home that is a fusion of architecture and the outdoors.

The topography dominates the views inside this house, too. Light reflecting the red earth of the butte floods the interior, turning everything pink—a challenge for interior designer Jill Jones. "The colors must either be integrated or confronted," she says. "We chose buckskin and krista khaki tones to defy the pink reflection."

Above – An undulating adobe wall softens the desert landscape. Left – Good desert architecture takes advantage of sun-beams that telegraph through windows and sky-lights.

Large boulders help define indoor/outdoor elements in this desert home. This surprise element brings a dimension of interest to a curved hallway. The languid, fluid motion is mimicked by a custom-made alder credenza.

Left – Local craftsmen understand the native vegetation and incorporate it in their work. Willow grows strong and tall quite easily in the desert environment. On this cabinet, willow is not only sturdy but visually appealing. Right – Looking more like a piece of furniture than a bathroom counter, this hand-built cabinet has the mass and proportion to suit the weight and substance suggested by the tile. Far more than elementary art projects, copper engraved panels are paintings in metal.

Features throughout the desert home constantly point toward integrating nature as part of everyday life. Substantial glass doors built on a sliding track system disappear into walls, blurring the boundaries between outdoor patios, sitting room, and kitchen. All windows face northeast for the best cooling and a view of long, interesting shadows across the landscape.

Shades of the desert paint the home furnishings with earthy colors, inspire shapes, and suggest textures. Slate floors, sealed plaster walls, solid wood cabinets, and free-form furniture reflect the colors of the jumbo stones governing the house. "We use local craftsmen who know the indigenous materials and finishes that are most compatible with the climatic conditions," says furniture designer Sherry

A penumbra of log corbels line the ceiling in this art gallery entrance. From a vast outdoor space into a vast indoor one, from nature's painting into the creative mind of man, here is a hallway that gives meaning to the term *grand entrance.*

Right – The theme of natural materials is personified on this kitchen counter. Bark remains on the willow where feet may kick the surface. Below – Copper is the material of the twenty-first century. Its warmth, beauty, and color has changed the face of the kitchen. Here a pounded copper sink is sunk into a marble countertop like a piece of jewelry.

Thompson. The willow around the kitchen bar and guest bathroom was gathered from the surroundings and installed by skilled carpenters who understand the properties of the material. The copper sconces, copper hood over the kitchen stove, and other copper accessories carry the stamp of local patterns, designs, and patina finishes. Most unusual are the mountain-shaped copper bands on the wrought-iron entrance gate. This inspired silhouette is etched on the doorbell and repeated

glass and sculptures placed throughout the house in unexpected places.

Many rooms in the house make resourceful use of space. The den and media room each double as a guest room. A Murphy bed ingeniously hides behind a sliding bookshelf or a film screen, revealing a painting on the wall when lowered. "We didn't want the media room to look like a media room so guests could also feel comfortable in it as a bedroom," Thompson explains.

The media room is a special showplace. The combination of offbeat light fixtures, plaster with a copper patina, and angular colored-glass windows makes an artistic statement rather than a utilitarian one. The sofa may seem to occupy an oddball
position, but placing the sofa on a platform puts film viewers above the heads of
those seated in the chairs below.

Most people want to live in an oasis, not in a harsh desert; in this way the
Moenkopi House is the perfect example of desert-style living. One can unite with
nature sheltered by a wall of windows, become lost in a film deep in the interior of
the home, or enjoy the evening coolness beside a tumbling stream of recycled water.
Jones loves living in the desert "because the scenery is so spectacular and I find that
reflective and calming. Climate-wise, you have to be agreeable to it, and I prefer heat."
The desert is in bloom nine months out of the year. Who couldn't live with that?

Left – Guests can be regally entertained in this commanding home theater. A sofa raised on a platform above the leather chairs in the foreground allows guests to view a screen uninhibited. Right – This cavernous rock formation was moved from the mountains seen in the background to serve as the perfect outdoor fireplace. Desert evenings can be cool and a fire is just the right primitive touch under the stars.

5 | OPEN INTERIOR SPACES

and Vaulted Ceilings

This adobe and stone house is not perched atop a mountain—it is an extension of desert elements. The fine surface of the adobe and the contrasting texture of the stone are an extraordinary match to the surroundings. In fact, the stone right outside the house is a perfect match to the stone on the house.

A touch of Tuscany in the desert is not out of character. Venetian plaster, a work of craftsmanship in Italy, translates easily into this desert home.

Even the pressed concrete walkway was carefully stained to blend with and complement its surroundings. The wrought-iron balustrade and Spanish-tile roof distinctly personalize this home with old-world character.

Living in the high desert is vastly different than living on the low desert floor where yucca grows from the sand. Here, a mini-forest of desert piñon and junipers surrounds the house, and wildflowers grow amongst granite boulders. Instead of mild weather changes, there are four distinct seasons. Although it doesn't get uncomfortably cold during winter, there is some snow. That doesn't happen in the low desert.

But, it is still the desert after all, and the glaring light and heat must be dealt with. Intense sunlight reflecting from stone and soil can be harsh and wearing.

Left – Old-world charm is married with an updated southwestern look in this high desert home. Wrought-iron balustrades, desert stone, and adobe intermingle perfectly. A counterpoint of curves and angles balances the design elements. The inviting curved walkway is stained the natural color of the earth. Right – The entrance to this high-desert home immediately suggests Tuscany with the warm, irregular surface of Venetian plaster. An Italian glass chandelier, the embossed antique mirror, and a Spanish Colonial chair all suggest an old-world heritage in the southwest.

Consequently, a home that is cavernous and dark feels cool and mollifies the heat, inviting relaxation.

The warm colors on the interior walls of this home remind one of a Tuscany manor. Both old-world and southwestern design can be used to create desert style. Here the two are mixed, a beguiling blend in the roomy spaces.

"I love Italy," the owner says. "Tuscany is hot and dry also. The homes are large with high ceilings and coven arches. We wanted something of a rich terra-cotta color in the rooms, but not quite as dark." This was achieved by combining color pigments with stucco and aged lime in a method known as Venetian plaster. The trowel is dragged across the plaster, giving the appearance of ancient striated stones. A glaze or wax is applied and polished as with the frescoes of the Renaissance. The intent is not to have a perfect finish, but rather to achieve the look of an old Spanish villa.

Coven arches distinguish old-world architecture like no other feature. Architects of the Spanish and Italian Renaissance borrowed the look from the Moors. They used arches as strong, structural weight-bearing passageways. Arches in early southwestern history remain true to this feature, which also keeps the use of timber—which is scarce in the desert—to a minimum. The arches in this home lend a graceful charm. A semicircular breakfast niche bends into a garden, and one can read the morning paper nestled among juniper trees.

Above – Common spaces that are open and uncluttered easily accommodate family gatherings. Left – Massive wooden doors gracefully and tactfully close off the privacy of a home office. Venetian plaster in a variegated terra-cotta distinguishes the surface as it did in the Renaissance era.

A large family and a multitude of friends dictate spacious open rooms where everyone can spread out. The large farm table in the dining room seats ten people, and no one is elbow to elbow. In fact, the table is surrounded with Spanish chairs

Right – State-of-the-art appliances fit for a restaurateur punctuate the warm colors of Tuscany in this spacious kitchen. A pounded copper hood etched with rivets sets the tone of the kitchen. Countertops, preparation centers, and a breakfast-counter balance the design. Wide-open to a cozy breakfast nook, formal dining room, and family room, the space is inviting and accessible. Left – A chipped stone sink in the guest bathroom is reminiscent of early Roman archeology. This timeworn texture contrasts the smooth glassy finish of a granite countertop. The framed wall-to-wall mirror gives the small room an illusion of spaciousness.

Left – Ribbed beams span this 14 foot ceiling in the dining room. Heat rises up and away from the table, allowing a more comfortable temperature below. The arched nook is perfect for a confectioner's table where coffee is served. A Venetian painting on Italian tiles is the only art needed for this dining room. Right – Artistic bird feeders surround the house, hanging from juniper trees. Outdoor furniture surrounds the house on terraces and patios, offering multiple options to watch the wildlife.

shaped and sized for a royal gathering. The raised ceiling allows the room to cool as heat rises. The ribbed beams add mass and a touch of natural wood that offsets the organic appearance of the Venetian plaster.

The kitchen has an obvious Tuscan feel. The owner, a restaurateur, wanted an inspired space to invent full-bodied cuisine. The design feels ethereal, incorporating fervid sunset colors. The stain-resistant and easily cleaned salmon-colored marble counters are elegant and practical too. The glow of copper faucets resonates with Italian history, where copper piping dates back to early Roman times. A pounded copper hood edged with studs hovers over the professional stove, a sculptural element with a function.

Outside living is important to the family's way of life. Wrought-iron terraces, backyard patios, and garden seating areas appear around the house and in the trees. The owner laughs, "Since living in this kind of space was a long time coming for our family, we like to joke about where we are going to sit tonight. Which terrace? we ask ourselves."

Everywhere in the yard hang birdbaths, fountains, and feeding stations to attract wildlife. A number of trees hug the house so closely that one wonders if the branches might not one day reach in and join the family.

PHOTO BY MARY WHITESIDES

6 | COLOR AND TEXTURE

Designer Paul Faulk prefers a cave-like feeling in his desert home. He calls it his nest. After being out in public running around in the sun, he nestles at home in deep rich colors and lush textured Spanish furnishings. "Dark colors help me survive the constant glare. The darker the color, the richer the room feels."

Desert living suits Faulk well. "I love the heat of the desert. Cold-weather places—I prefer to be a visitor." The granddaddy saguaros and resilient succulents alone make the desert primitive. "The blooms on cactus are remarkable—new life springs from ancient growth," he says. Sometimes the heat and lack of moisture even gets to these indomitable plants and hinders flowering. Faulk is undaunted.

PHOTO BY MARY WHITESIDES

Spanish Colonial architecture is an important legacy of the southwestern states. The umber colors and textures of chipped plaster are as valued today as a family heirloom.

"A drip system is a must. I wouldn't miss the showy blossoms even in times of drought."

The philosophy for the interior of Faulk's home is also tied to the ancient cactus landscape. It suggests creating an age-old look and nourishing it with a drip system of color and texture. Weathered furnishings have character and tell stories. Good design has contrast but he doesn't use color for that. Furniture that blends into the room and envelops makes more sense. A dark piece of furniture on a white wall can be bothersome, so he looks to texture to execute the principle of contrast. A marble table is offset by a carved mirror, velvets are paired with leather, and a rusted chandelier meets with silver candlesticks and a collection of fine crystal. These types of contrasts distinguish Faulk's brand of desert style. "Cracks or chipping of paint don't bother me either. New things look plastic," he says.

Since he is a designer who works with so many different tastes, Faulk turns homeward to reclaim his essence. Soft lighting provides a restful environment, one that is inviting to the soul. "My house is an evening house. Even on the weekends it is restful and peaceful. I love being surrounded by my collections."

A pyramid of antique glass globes greets the desert light through an open door. Bubbles

and fissures catch a coruscation of beams, making the entire room sparkle and glow. Faulk has other collections, such as a group of primitive magnifying glasses with hand-chiseled glass, held together with rawhide strings. His many clay urns come from Turkey, Greece, Mexico, Spain, and Morocco. The shapes and textures of the urns and the fact that they were handmade out of clay and dirt attracted Faulk. "They were functional in their time. The more aged and distressed they are, the more I like them." The design principles of aged and distressed materials are carried throughout the house.

The 1,900-square-foot house, redone in 1981, had the contrived faux finishes of that period. Standard ceiling and wall textures typical at that time needed to be

Left – Rich, warm umber tones mollify the glaring heat of the desert in this bedroom. The curlicue twists and turns on the bed pay dramatic homage to early Spanish craftsmen, while the simplicity of an antique mission chest perfectly offsets the ornamental ironwork. Right – Rich brocades, fringed pillows, Spanish silver, and fine crystal collections are judicious choices for an authentic old-world décor.

honed to Faulk's taste. "I actually painted the entire house with three quarts of paint," he says. The end result was intended to appear as though the process was not worked at. He used three different shades of peach terracotta paint and mixed water into it. Starting with the darkest color, a terry-cloth rag was used to dab the paint in random splotches. The second lighter shade, watered down as well, was also applied randomly. The lightest shade, watered to a thin consistency, was washed over the entire wall, subtly blending in the patchy edges. A glaze then sealed the process, adding an old-world patina.

The house changes frequently, sometimes as often as every three months. In order not to fail at a client's house, Faulk uses his own house as the test. "New ideas are tried here first. My failure rate is lower that way," he explains. He has recently decided not to make any more changes to the guest bedroom.

The rooms in the house are not large but they flow well, which is important when entertaining. Dinner parties are small and intimate. The guests are so embraced by the dining room that they don't want to leave. The table is a large square surrounded by oversized chairs and benches, making conversation easy. Everyone stays involved, not like with a rectangular table where those at the far ends may have a harder time joining in. Lighting is placed on dimmers to add mystery and romance, and a multitude of candles are lit. "We never put an ending time on our parties. People leave when they are tired," Faulk remarks. The longer guests stay, the more

Collections personalize a home more than any other element. These antique glass balls full of bubbles and fissures were not valued highly in their day. Today, they are a rare find, and newly made ones try to emulate the imperfections of the originals.

Contrasts are the measure of good interior design. Many colors and textures comingle in this dining room, adding a warm invitation to guests. An elegant chandelier hangs from a barn-wood ceiling, a cluster of earthen pots sit atop a luxurious brocade table cover, and rusted curlicue iron accentuates a fine oil painting.

comfortable they are, and that is the measure of a successful gathering.

Christmas is a major event in this household. Half of the furniture is hauled out to accommodate fourteen decorated trees, which are worked into the rooms so that you hardly know they are there. Each year is a new theme. Last year's old-world trees, decorated in different colors and antique baubles, brought three hundred people through the house over the course of a weekend. "It was marvelous," Faulk says. "And that's what home is all about."

FURNİTURE AND DECOR

The interweaving of eclectic accessories and classic furniture comes together in a single narrative in this desert-style bungalow renovation. Interior designer Jo Taulbee loves the Spanish Colonial pieces she brought with her from New Mexico. The sparse look of primitive furniture calls for a layer of antique silver or a bevy of candles and crystals. The ice-cool reflections catch light in a magical way. "I am fascinated by desert light and the way it makes love to the curves in adobe, enters the windows in the morning, highlights ochre walls and paintings, shoots across the floor, and disappears in the late afternoon," she says. Taulbee is always cognizant of such beauty, placing appropriate objects in light paths.

Taulbee's talent for finding special accessories and antiques invests the room with personality as though a designer never entered the house. "I like to place a

Left – Finding one unusual piece of furniture that no one else has can set the décor apart. This carved antique shelf is unlike any found in the contemporary market. Sublimely set off by a magnificent embossed silver mirror, this entrance is truly personalized and welcoming.

beautifully carved chair where least expected." Or she may mix something grand from the Colonial era with elegant hand-painted velvet. She peruses junk stores, flea markets, and antique shops to find Brazilian crystals, old boxes and photographs, old fountains, and anything with an aura of history that is tactile and radiates a tangible feel. A pair of mirrors from a castle in Spain was purchased on the spur of the moment, along with two gilded chairs.

Taulbee interviews her clients extensively to find the perfect way to express their own personal desert style. Plans are made, but at a certain point the house dictates its own direction. Never forgetting scale, dramatic lighting, and texture, she uses these cohesive elements to assure congruity in design and client satisfaction. To fine-tune all

Left – A Spanish bungalow built in the 1970s is transformed by shrubs, potted plants, and terra-cotta tiles. Right – One very special piece of furniture used as a focal point is window dressing for the rest of the room. This rare antique colonial chair came from an estate in Europe. The refined armoire behind it is an exquisite example of early Spanish craftsmanship.

her projects, Taulbee consults her feng shui master. "An environment should be alive, not static. It just has to be done right," insists Taulbee. "Old pieces liven the atmosphere and in a clean setting, the chi flows."

Color can also be used to highlight and manipulate space. "Some people think they should use all white, but forget how harsh the glare from the sun can be," Taulbee

says from experience. "I think we should chose soft muted colors that are like a balm in our heat." Any detail that suggests cool belongs in the desert. Antique white linens are an exception to the white theory; this is one element in which white suggests cool.

Above – The right mix of antique and contemporary furnishings, with ornate accents, is a key design secret in desert style. Left – Designed by Jo Taulbee, this colonial-inspired bowl is crafted in South America. Right – The monks in early Santa Fe commissioned Spanish craftsmen to train Native Americans in the art of furniture making. Out of that training emerged a simpler version of Spanish Colonial furniture. This armoire is an example of that style and shows the inner beauty and detail of an early piece.

Far left – A Spanish Colonial stool with cabriole legs is upholstered with hand-painted leather in a Native American graphic. Candles always bring warmth to a room and are used here in lieu of a crackling fire. Left – A gilded mirror from a castle in Europe differentiates this room in a way no other mirror can. Below – Antique Turkish pots that functioned hundreds of years ago as water jugs are now retired at the foot of a bed as pure form and embellishment.

Colors used in desert interiors should translate to the exteriors with the fabrics on draperies and outdoor furniture, as well as choices for plants and pots. Patios and gardens should not be considered a separate entity but an integral part of the interior. An old cast-stone fireplace mantel used most often indoors is set against a wall on the patio. Lit candles glow at night as the sun sets across the desert expanse.

"No rooftops obscure my view. Looking off my back patio I see the mountains, palo verdé trees, and saguaro cactus," says Taulbee. She likes the raucous call of the coyote and has a reverence for animals. "Watching a coyote on the horizon in the early morning hours or catching

the antics of a Harris hawk while walking my dog is like being in the wilderness but in civilization," she says. Morning is a good time for outdoor activities in the desert. The summer months turn people nocturnal; learning to cope with the heat of the day is essential to desert-style living.

Left – Soft taupe walls help soften the glare of harsh desert light. Fresh white antique linens accent the whimsy of an iron bed. Right – A fireplace mantel used out of context in an outdoor room spawns imaginative desert evenings. Pergola-type beams filter desert light, shading the patio without totally obstructing the sun or a full moon.

8 | INCORPORATING WATER

This gray concrete structure lies prone and sculptural on the site, as if it were zipped to the desert floor. "Such neutralizing color seems to camouflage and adapt to the different changes of sunrise, sunset, and landscape," says Hector Ramirez, architect. He planned the undulating layout so cleverly that it traces the shapes of the mountains and mesas of the setting. "There is a familiar feeling while walking in or out of this home that flows and draws towards nature."

Sudden rainstorms in the desert can cause flash floods. A rusted chain called a *cadenzas scupper* helps direct rainwater into a recycle system to water plants and feed a stream near the house.

Copper and wooden fascia roofs provide shade and shadow. They are adorned with a rusted chain called a *cadenzas scupper,* used in medieval times to direct water from a sudden rainfall. The entry door is a work of art inspired by the contours of the desert. With its abstract shapes, copper inset, and peep window, it is an elegant welcome to the house.

A scintillating mosaic fountain greets guests entering this Arizona home.
Shimmering water washes over luminous colors of patterned tiles and precious
stones, instantly lifting the visitor's spirits. The mountainous sculpture, so unexpected in the desert atmosphere, gives this residence a "wow" factor. The fountain
is a creative collaboration of the owner, architect, artist, and interior designer.

"This cupola and traga-luces sculpture pays tribute to the crumpled ten-foot granite outcropping near the house," says Ramirez. "It is the heart of the home, and the sound of soothing water is felt in every room like an oasis." Gems lie randomly placed and translucent beneath the cascading water.

Interior designer Jo Taulbee saw bright gems gleaming in the Madi Kohla River.

"It was an image that stayed with me from a trek in Nepal," she says. "All the stones had washed down into the riverbeds, which were full of garnets and floating ice." Taulbee wanted this kind of light and color in the fountain, so artist John Barren placed the gems just right. Being cognizant of how the water would run down the fountain and over the gems required a calculated curvature. Well-placed garnets, amethysts, and embossed tiles glisten in the backlit fountain much the same as the gems in the Nepalese river scene.

The floor plan masterfully segregates the house into four major sections. Each branch has two intersections where desert light and architecture fuse. Windows and skylights orchestrate a light show throughout the rooms, casting shadows and enriching interior colors. The great room—the core of the house—is an emporium of public spaces. It embraces the dining room, hugs the kitchen, and gives a home to the entertainment center. Guests and family can stretch out here to watch a film or take a meal by the fireplace. Noise from this public area is isolated from the master suite, guest bedrooms, and children's wing.

The compelling art choices and the elegant old-world furnishings complement the architecture perfectly. Contrasted elements of color and texture connect the furnishings to the house. Light and dark colors provide a strong palette for the furnishings. Fresh off-white plaster walls reach from organic snapped slate floors to a rich brown wooden ceiling of distressed vigas. The vibrant orange tones in the paintings, the subtle green and

Above – A Native American bronze may seem paradoxical in front of a Spanish Colonial mirror but in fact adds dimension to desert history and contemporary art. Below – This Spanish Colonial bed is made by Mexican craftsmen who studied the art in Spain. The traditional pattern is applied in gold leaf. Black has a restful, cool affect perfect for the bedroom. Right – This desert-style home is segregated into four distinct wings. The great room is the central point connecting these sections. Herringbone-patterned vigas contrast soft chamois colored walls and snapped slate floors.

Left – Guests can freshen up in this bathroom while gazing into an old-world silver-framed mirror and rinse their hands in mosaic artistry. Below – The architecture of this desert-style home silhouettes the lines and shapes of the mountains behind. Its concrete color also helps it blend with its surroundings, minimizing visibility. Right – A negative-edge pool seems to merge with the desert floor, leading the eye to the mountain views. A Jacuzzi in the center of the pool is not only well designed graphically but functional as well. It brings truth to the old adage "form follows function."

rose colors of the upholstered Spanish dining chairs, and the soft corn-yellow hue of the sofa are bluntly punctuated by a black coffee table, tying together the boundaries between yin and yang. This is a house where rectilinear lines meet curved ones, where silver tea sets are decorously placed under rusted metal chandeliers, and a cast bronze Indian encounters an antique gilded mirror. These distinguishing contrasts bear a strong similarity to the owners' philosophy, whose main residence is in a major city. Their desert home combines the perfect essence of grandeur, spaciousness, and quietude—a balance to the

stimulus of the irascible traffic and stressful demands of city living.

The sweeping view of vigilant mountains and cactus help soothe city stress. Across the patio a negative-edge pool channels the eye to valleys and peaks. Privacy barriers shield the outdoor living space from adjoining neighbors, and a sunken fire pit offers warmth after a chilly evening swim.

INCORPORATING ART

PHOTO BY KATSUHISA KIDA

T his house is a lesson in site and art dictating function. The owners are fervent collectors and wanted a way to live amongst glass sculptures and fine art. Their goal: to live on nature's desert canvas in an artistic way. Architects Bing Hu and Erik Peterson listened carefully to the needs of their clients and designed a home around their art and the landscape. As a result, niche shelves and walls are measured spaces providing backdrops for displaying the owners' extensive art collection. The rest of the architecture is an umbrella of angles and shapes inspired by the site.

An umbrella of angles and shapes architecturally inspired by the site is seen here in the roofline of this Phoenix home. It hovers over an infinity-edge pool, inviting a nighttime swimmer to view the stars.

The house nestles between the gigantic boulders that other residents of the neighborhood look up to see. The home quietly shares the landscape and mimics the surrounding area. Quartzite stone used on the home is in the same varied shades as

the landscape—mushroom gray, buff, and tan. Stone pillars used throughout the house are the connecting webs from ground level to roof, between windows and walls, interiors and exteriors. Curved rooflines break the hard edges of an otherwise angular building. There is an intersection of various wall and ceiling planes not unlike the natural shapes of the desert.

The interior spaces are designed to have a very open feel so that one can drink

PHOTO BY KATSUHISA

Left – Art and sculpture are immediately apparent from the first approach to the front entrance of this desert-style home. The home is a statement for living with art. Above right – The curvature of a stone retaining wall and the negative-edge pool give the illusion of a waterfall to neighbors below. Below right – The kitchen is the grand central gathering place of the home. TV viewers are made comfortable in overstuffed chairs. An abstract patterned rug, designed specifically for this space, is inspired by desert topography. A lengthy curved counter is a luxurious place to lounge over, sip a drink, or converse with the chef.

in the desert environment. A neutral color scheme selected by interior designer Paula Berg quietly defines the bold and colorful art, architecture, and desert vista. A sand-colored floor of French limestone runs indoors and outdoors, providing a connecting color palette to all areas of the house. Rift-cut bleached-oak ceilings extend the light, airy ambience. Blackened steel beams accent the flush lines of the ceiling and delineate the architectural edges.

Berg's sensitivity to people-comforts is not compromised by her superb design sense. She carefully assembles groupings of sumptuous sofas and chairs to encourage intimate conversation. See-through shelves inserted between stone pillars draw the eye

PHOTOS BY KATSUHISA KIDA

An enormous wall-to-wall window frames the formal dining room as though it is a piece of art. Stone columns function as shelves and balance the room on either side. The owners not only collect art; they live in it as well.

PHOTO BY KATSUHISA KIDA

The color accents in this artistic desert home come from glass-art collections, table settings, and oil paintings. The muted colors of walls, floors, and ceilings neither compete with the art nor the desert surroundings. See-through glass shelving maximizes space and visibility.

to art objects and through to the next room. Collections of fine art glass and paintings distinguish the owner's taste and feed the imagination. The dining room has volumes of space with unfettered views that include distant city lights at night. Berg custom-designed the stainless steel–and–glass table. A special patina colors the steel a shade of charcoal, linking the metal finish to the structural accents of the home.

A kitchen with a lowered arched ceiling is the heart of the home. With deep sienna pear-wood cabinets backlit by warm display lights, it is a relaxing offset to the formal areas of the house. A neutral-colored granite counter rallies people together as would a luxuriant lunch counter. Low voltage lighting sends a soft wash across the ceiling. Clerestory windows balance the room with natural light. Across the room, twin overstuffed chairs and ottomans sit before a big-screen TV on a striated wool carpet. Multiyarns woven together with no visible seams depict an abstract desertscape.

An outdoor dining room with fireplace and wet bar is easily accessible through the kitchen. Desert nights are seductive invitations to dine in the open air, and somehow the fresh air enhances the flavor of a meal.

The master suite backs up against large boulders as if in the lap of sleeping giants. The owners like to cozy up in the privacy of their own wing and soak in the adjacent spa after a day of entertaining. Three bedroom suites and a family room located in a separate wing of the house allow guests the luxury of total privacy as well.

The balance of energy between desert and architecture has an incredible Zen-like influence on this house. Its peaceful uncluttered structure, accented with beautiful art, completely draws one into the environment.

Outdoor dining is just steps from the main kitchen. A grill, seating area, and dining table bring a dimension of outdoor desert living to the home.

10 | THE DESERT IN BLOOM

Many people view the desert landscape as barren and desolate, yet the seasons, rains, and arroyos can change this viewpoint overnight. Unexpected rain can coax a cactus flower to bloom, send a flash flood to create a river, and end a seven-year sleep cycle for Mexican poppies. The ancient Indians found many wild resources for clothing, homes, furniture, fuel, and food in the so-called desert wasteland, and their forefathers even became farmers. Agriculture began in the deserts.

These cultivated saguaro cacti will be a century old by the time they reach the height of their wild relatives growing in the open desert. The bloom is rare and lasts only a day or two.

Yet the drastic climate of the desert, with its extreme heat and cold, sandy soil, and lack of water is a challenge to agriculture, landscaping, and gardening. These challenges must be overcome to make the desert bloom.

The desert is the home to such wildlife as the coyote, rodents, snakes, spiders, and a number of birds. The landscape is a painting of alluvial fans, water pocket folds, arroyos, buttes, mesas, and flat lands in an assortment of colors and vegetation. Plant life in the desert has qualities that make it adaptive to drought. The vegetation in low deserts includes cacti, succulents, and wildflowers. The vegetation in the high desert includes juniper, piñon, sage, and rabbit brush.

Cacti are always succulents but succulents are not always cacti. Both species thrive in the desert because of their ability to store moisture in roots, stems, or leaves over long periods of time. They also thrive in a variety of environments because of spines and tough skins resistant to pests and predators. Luxuriant flowers of these plants last only a short while and refuse to bloom when water is scarce. The flowers enjoy an

An unusually thick bed of aloe saponaria thrives under the armed branches of an oak tree. The flowers look very much like a lily. The saponaria is a member of the succulent family. These prolific plants require little water and brighten a garden without much effort on the part of the gardener.

This plant is a member of the aloe agave genus of succulents. Growing here in a semiarid high-desert atmosphere, it receives more rain than the same plants in the low desert—thus the gigantic size. The Native Americans used a species of agave plant as food. When peeled, pulped, and cooked in a fire pit, it tastes like sweet potato. The flowers can be boiled and eaten or dried for use in soups, stews, or gumbo. Seeds can be ground into flour.

austere backdrop without leaves, making them the spectacular feature of the plant.

Cacti come in a variety of shapes, sizes, and colors. They have different blooms and are endlessly adapting to wind, rain, drought, and erosion. Cacti morph into different shapes, looking like timeless sculptures formed beyond the wildest thoughts of a human sculptor. These plants can be fluted, rounded, free-formed, treelike, and humanlike. Cacti threaten animals, insects, and other predators with spiny thorns, but they also nourish with edible pads, fruits, and stalks. They have survived forty

million years through weather conducive to extinction. Succulents grow in all parts of the world, but cacti are native only to the western hemisphere.

The wily cactus flower can be difficult to witness. Many bloom at night; others for short periods in the day. Some blooms last only twenty-four hours and have strong vanilla fragrances to attract pollinating bugs. Many people are interested in witnessing desert blooms and there is even a hot line in many areas to check for blooming times. Many cacti are on the endangered species list; they are easily destroyed in their fragile growth conditions. A special police force in Arizona patrols the desert in search of cacti poachers.

Succulents horde water in bulging leaves, and come in shapes resembling flowers, trees, cabbages, ruffles, and berries. The legendary agave, or century plant, has many uses. Sisal fibers stripped from their tall thin stalks are used to make rope, mats, and carpets. Tequila made from the Tequilana Agave is one of the largest enterprises in Mexico. Cultivating peyote, a dumpling-shaped aloe, is prohibited because of its strong hallucinatory powers. Other friendly succulents without spines have medicinal

Left – This saguaro cactus, the granddaddy of all cactus plants, is at least one hundred years old. It is capable of surviving droughts for years by sending out a deep root system. The saguaro blooms in late March or early April in the Sanoran desert; the flower lasts only one day, but desert sleuths are adept at catching the show. Below – A member of the Christmas cactus family, this huge flower is known as the cactus orchid. The flowers can reach a diameter of 10 inches and come in several glorious colors, including red, pink, orange, and white.

PHOTO BY MARY WHITESIDES

properties as well as culinary uses.

Desert wildflowers will blossom depending on the percentage of rainfall. Hardy plants, such as the wild Mexican poppy, will sometimes lay dormant for seven-year periods. It last bloomed in 2001, flooding the desert floor with an orange carpet. Countless species bloom again after a dormant spell of twelve to twenty months. The mysterious recovery and survival of these flowers in harsh conditions attract horti-culturists, flower lovers, and camera buffs—like sleuths tracking great treasures.

Piñon pine, juniper, sage, and rabbit brush grow in upper elevations. Piñon nuts are a gourmet treat that sell for exorbitant prices in boutique food shops. But for the ancient aboriginal peoples, pine nuts were an essential part of their diet. The time of harvest was a reverent social gathering of family and friends.

The giant Joshua tree is found nowhere else in the world but the Mojave desert. South of St. George, Utah, you will see this tree scattered along the desert floor. In Arizona, you will find a forest of giant Joshua trees. To catch this forest in bloom is sublime.

Cacti are always succulents, but succulents are not always cacti. Succulents have the distinct ability to morph into shapes only an artist could imagine. This cabbage-like succulent holds enough water to make the leaves puff; if punctured it will bleed water. Succulents send out stems and baby plants that can be replanted to propagate a whole new plant.

PHOTO BY MARY WHITESIDES

The barrel cactus holds water much like a sponge and has large red flowers that bloom from the top. It is an edible cactus if prepared correctly. The pulp is bitter, but when boiled with sugar it tastes like watermelon preserves. Because of this it has earned the nickname "candy cactus."

Growing desert plants, even under controlled conditions, can be trying. But with knowledge and understanding, harsh winds, extreme temperatures, difficult soils, and lack of moisture can be dealt with. And once a cultivated system is in place, maintenance is simple.

TIPS FOR DESERT-STYLE GARDENS

Working with Mother Nature rather than against her tends to create successful solutions. Each area of the country has its own local conditions and problems. Study the requirements for desert gardening in your area to save time and resources and ensure a successful, thriving garden.

Desert soil is alkaline and low in phosphates. To correct the pH balance, add phosphate mixed in organic matter. Desert soil is usually clay and has a cement-textured crust called *caliche*. Caliche, located about six to twelve inches from the surface, is a silt-sand build-up that seals itself when water is applied. Adding sulfur compounds can be effective in penetrating the soil. Raised flowerbeds are a good solution as well.

Soil crusting and weeds take extra water. By mixing soil with nutrients, mulch, and topsoil you can help the soil stay moist. Pulling thirsty weeds will preserve moisture for the plants you grow by choice. You can control drifting sands by ground cover to secure soil and by creating barriers with rows of bushes to divert the wind. Using native species is a must; intensified heat during the summer months parches plants that are not meant for desert climates. The season for planting is in the fall when temperatures cool down. Avoid planting near westerly walls and windows and always water in the cooler part of evening to minimize evaporation.

Some sedum and sempervivum succulents survive cold winters and northern humidity; they create interesting ground cover that stabilizes fragile soils. Cactus plants grow easily from cuttings and offsets. Joint, stem, or leaf cuttings taken from the parent plant can produce new plants without much effort. Place the cut portion into a

Left – Water features in the desert are man's attempt at creating an oasis. Some deserts are deceiving as to their lack of water; they have underground lakes known as aqua fir that make water less of an issue. When water is scarce, it is important that it be recycled on a pump system. Right – This mountain wildflower-like plant is known as hellianthum and grows easily in drought conditions. In addition to the beauty of the delicate purple flower it is the perfect ground cover to help stabilize the soils and shifting desert sands.

A variety of cacti and succulents planted among
bushy goldeneye make a
pleasing garden. Governed
by Xeriscape methods of
gardening, this landscape
will virtually take care of
itself. The organ-pipe cactus will get tiny red flowers
around the tip and the
aloe will shoot up big bell-
like flowers in the spring.
Goldeneye, a member of
the sunflower family,
bushes out if trimmed
properly.

PHOTO BY MARY WHITESIDES

The juniper tree grows only in a high desert climate, where the precipitation increases enough to sustain the evergreen quality of the tree. Edible juniper berries are used by German cooks to flavor sauerkraut and cabbage and by the French in stews. Americans use the berries to flavor wild game.

mixture of sand and perlite, then water and let it dry so roots form before replanting. Replant in sand and potting soil. Offsets are new plants connected to the mother plant by umbilical cord–like extensions. Baby shoots from the chicken succulent, for instance, produce roots and can be transplanted as separate plants.

You can grow strong, sturdy plants by using a broadleaf P4 in the soil to help retain moisture. The substance remains active for five years and will protect trees, shrubs, and flowers from drought stress.

Look into the principles of Xeriscaping—a water-conservation method for western gardens. The word is coined from the Greek *xeri* meaning dry. Following are several principles of Xeriscape that can help you when planning a desert-style garden.

1. Use plants and grasses that are native to your area.

2. Limit the size of lawn areas.

3. Add organic matter like compost to help the soil hold moisture. Add mulch to shade the soil and keep it cool.

4. Don't overwater. Use soaker hoses and drip irrigation.

5. Don't use high-nitrogen fertilizers that will create lush, overgrown plants that need a lot of water.

Keep an eye on your flowering plants for dead or dying blooms. It is important to remove the dead growth to encourage new blooms and growth. This procedure will also prevent the reseeding of aggressive plants you wish to control.

While the dictionary may define *desert* as barren and sparsely occupied, humankind challenges that idea. Amenities such as gardens and water features can be built into desert-style living. After all, the oasis is the mythical mirage of desert stories, and humans have a way of making fantasy into reality.

HOW-TO TIPS

There are many different ways to implement desert style into your home. Your own individual style and taste will be reflected in your choices. The following are a few suggestions for incorporating specifics of desert style.

ENTRANCE

The front door is the first impression of your home; it provokes interest in what lies beyond. Give voice to a door by treating it as a means to facilitate hospitality. Use it as a welcome sign on which to hang your personal style.

Many companies manufacture a wide variety of doors. Pinecrest has one of the most comprehensive and original selections of front doors. Constructed of

PHOTO BY LYDIA CUTTER

solid wood, hand carved, inlaid with beveled glass, and fronted with curlicue iron, they create many different looks to serve many different needs. To spare the expense of a new door, you can use a basic wooden door and then antique, stud with metal, ornately hinge, or dress it up with a fine doorknob. Old doors can be painted, sandblasted, stained in a graphic pattern, appliqued with accents, and embossed. Express yourself with your door and imbue it with the soul of your home. First impressions are lasting impressions.

WOOD

The warmth of aged woods exemplifies the essence of old-world, whether used as flooring or as touches added to a ceiling. Reclaimed wood is an excellent way to authenticate an antique look. Many companies deal in reclaimed lumber from dismantled barns, factories, and various commercial buildings. Train trestle wood is a popular choice for accents such as lintels on windows and doors, or beams to add mass in a dining room. To maintain the integrity of aged wood, a waxed and polished finish rather than varnish or Polyurethane is recommended.

Another way to achieve the look of aged wood is to purchase third-grade planks and lay them out as flooring. Third-grade wood has knots and fissures normally

PHOTO BY ERIKA BLUMENFELD

associated with reclaimed wood. One of the most authentic ways to age wood is to use a mixture of mud and lime. Paint the mixture on the floor, and within twenty-four hours the floor will be antique. This method requires experimentation, and cleanup can be a challenge. A wooden floor can also be dry-brushed. By using very little paint on the tip of the brush you can get minimal coverage by stroking and dragging the brush across the floor. Try light crème colors on dark woods or brown colors on lighter woods. This adds texture and interest to the wood because bits of paint are trapped in the imperfections. If you accidentally use too much paint, wipe and rub immediately with a rag. Some flooring experts paint floors black, sand them down, and finish with wax. If you don't mind a very rustic look try recycled scaffolding as flooring. Sanded and stained, it looks quite nice.

Framing pressed wood squares stained with multiple colors can enhance an ordinary ceiling. Pressed wood is available in comprehensive lumberyards and home improvement stores. For a simple rustic look, consider installing planks of antique wood on an alcove ceiling. Faux beams dressed with carved corbels instantly restate a room.

Finding a variety of tiles in the slush yard of a tile outlet provides an opportunity to be creative. Use a floor such as this as inspiration to come up with an interesting pattern of your own. It will require some cutting and fitting but in a small space such as an entrance, such artistry can set the tone of the house.

PHOTO BY MARY WHITESIDES

Concrete flooring is being used in all styles of homes from modern to rustic. Using a lightweight concrete mix can help alleviate weight-bearing problems. An inlaid pattern of rusted metal can further define desert style. In this floor, the iron pieces are set on spikes so that the concrete can flow around and below it. The concrete is then stained and waxed.

FLOORS

A concrete floor is a superb canvas for the ancient-contemporary, old-world, or updated southwestern desert style. Pouring concrete over existing floors and foundations can be a problem. Concrete needs to be a minimum of 2 inches thick to cure properly and resist cracking. The added mass can be a weight-bearing problem for an existing structure. Many new products on the market, such as Ardex Engineered Concrete, have created a mixture with lightweight binders that can be poured as thin as 1/2 inch and are self-leveling. They have the same properties as concrete, and look and act like concrete. By using stains you can achieve an overall warm mushroom color or use the many stain colors available to create patterns and textures. Rug effects with etched borders, inlaid tiles, or metal patterns offer endless possibilities to be original. If you don't want to bother with concrete, home improvement stores carry concrete tiles in varied colors.

If slate or limestone is not affordable, many home improvement stores have slush yards where small amounts of slate, limestone, or faux tiles can be purchased for a fraction of their original cost. Consider making a pattern in a variety of tiles with textures and colors similar to slate and limestone. Such an application is great in an entrance.

TEXTURED WALLS

Textured walls are a multifaceted art form ranging from involved Venetian plaster finishes to techniques that trick the eye. The tired look of faux painted and sponged walls has been abandoned for more authentic wall textures. Venetian plaster is an involved time-consuming process best left to well-trained craftsmen. To achieve a similar look, you can mix plaster to a semiliquid state—thin enough to be rolled on but thick enough to achieve a texture. Add color and roll on an imperfect surface. Plane the wall with a smoothing tool. To get the sheen of polished plaster, liquefy a can of neutral colored Bri Wax (leave it in the sun); add powdered pigments not well-mixed to attain color dimension. Place a car-polishing mitt on your hand and use it to dab wax on the wall. Polish with sheepskin or a chamois.

For textured accents, try covering one wall or your bookshelves with leather. Another material that can be used as flooring or on walls is cork. It has been greatly improved; through a new process it is now bug resistant and has a new resiliency and fine texture.

You can consult the many how-to books on finishes for more ideas. (See the resource directory on page 120.) Always ask an expert, experiment first, and make sure you are confident before using any technique.

FURNISHINGS

Furnishing a room can be daunting when you think of it in terms of all the pieces necessary to serve your needs. But well-designed rooms have one major focus that becomes the design impetus. Start with one spectacular piece of furniture that

PHOTO BY ERIKA BLUMENFELD

An ornate ceiling such as this can be a surprise design element in a desert home. Hand-carved wooden ceilings typical of old Spanish missions required precise craftsmanship. Many cut and carved ornamental wood pieces are available at local home improvement stores. Using imagination and a well-thought-out plan, a contemporary version can be created.

makes your heart sing. It is a piece that will reverberate around the room. You should be willing to spend a lot of money on this one item. An antique coffee table elaborately carved around the skirt will be a magnet drawing people to a conversation area.

Above – Personalize a home with collections. Items found in travels, made by friends, or found in antique shops add interest. These Chulucanas Indian pots are from Peru. The wave pattern on this hand-carved Peruvian sofa table symbolizes water and prosperity. Below – Search the antique shops and exclusive furniture stores for one very special piece of furniture that can distinguish the entire home. For example, using an antique coffee table with carved edges as a focal point will raise the perceived value of all the furnishings.

PHOTOS BY MARY WHITESIDES

Or an armoire may house your glass collection. Whatever other furnishings you bring into the room should be compatible and complementary. Well-chosen inexpensive components will be washed-over with an expensive imagination.

Above – A Chulucanas Indian–made pot is not only original in shape and pattern but has a history dating back hundreds of years. The pot is polished with a river stone and fired in mango leaves, giving it sheen like no other pottery. Right – The owner of this home collects antique pots from around the world. The pots, similar in shape and made using similar techniques, are a cross-cultural study. This pottery collection sparks conversation as well as adding a dramatic element to a desert-style home.

COLLECTIONS

Begin a collection of items that really interests you. Collections add personality to the home. *Santos* and *retablos* commonly found in desert homes are varied, artistic, and fascinating. Crosses are an art form and do not necessarily have to have a religious significance for the collector. Collections of glass direct light around the house through ribs, crystals, bubbles, and curves. Sculptures stand vigil in niches, guard hallways, enhance shelves, and reflect the creative mind of their maker. Art can paint the soul with emotion and imagination, invoking feelings of yearning, introspection, vibrancy, or calm. A unique sense of personal taste and design is expressed through accessories and collections.

CONCLUSION

Desert style has a wide range of expressions. By incorporating any or all of these ideas, you can create a home that reflects the elements of desert style and is uniquely you.

RESOURCES

ARCHITECTS

H & S International LLC
Bing Hu
17785 N. Pacesetter Way
Scottsdale, AZ 85255
Phone: (480) 585–6898
www.handsinternational.com

Kevin Kellogg, Architect
385 Watertrough
Sebastopol, CA 95404
Phone: (707) 829–3687
Architect experienced with rammed earth

Hector Ramirez
R + D Art Techs
10229 N. Scottsdale Rd. #D
Scottsdale, AZ 85253
Phone: (480) 368–0601
Fax: (480) 368–0621
Architecture sensitive to natural landscape

Jessie Whitesides, Architect
830 4th St.
Santa Rosa, CA 95404
Phone: (707) 569–9358

BOOKS ON FINISHES

The Complete Book of Decorating Techniques
By Linda Gray and Jocasta Innes
Published by Little, Brown

The Complete Guide to Painting and Decorating
By Black & Decker
Published by Creative Publishing, Inc.

Paint Recipes
By Liz Wagstaff
Published by Chronicle Books

Period Finishes and Effects
By Judith and Martin Miller
Published by Rizzoli

Recipes for Surfaces: A Fireside Book
By Mindy Drucker and Pierre Finkelstein
Published by Simon and Schuster

CROWN MOLDING

House of Fara
520 Eggebrecht Rd.
La Porte, IN 46350
Phone: (219) 362–8544; (800) 334–1732
www.houseoffara.com

In Ghana, Africa, a long tradition of bead-making inspired this unusual chandelier. Made of recycled glass and iron, it adds whimsical interest above a dining table. Designed by Phyllis Woods of Tribal Links.

Vintage Woodworks
Hwy 34 S – P.O. Box 39
Quinlan, TX 75474–0039
Phone: (903) 356–2158
Fax: (903) 356–3023
www.vintagewoodworks.com

HOME FURNISHINGS

Authentic Wood Floors
P.O. Box 153
Glen Rock, PA 17327
Phone: (717) 428–0904
Fax: (717) 428–0464
www.authenticwoodfloors.com
Recycled wood flooring

Borderlands Trading Company
Wes Baker
301 E. 7th St.
Tucson, AZ 85705
Phone: (520) 622–6454
Fax: (520) 622–8288
e-mail: BTC@earthlink.com
Rustic Mexican furniture and accessories

Casa Salazar Art Gallery
216 E. Houston St.
San Antonio, TX 78205
Phone: (210) 472–2272
www.themajestic.com/casa
Colonial furnishings

Colonial Arts
463 Union St.
San Francisco, CA 94133
Phone: (415) 505–0680
www.colonialarts.com
Arts, artifacts, and furniture

Droma Furniture
9520 S. W. 40th St.
Miami, FL 33165
Phone: (305) 223–3536; (800) 562–7940
Fax: (305) 223–9030
www.dromafurniture.com
Importers and exporters of colonial furniture

Michael Dumas
124 S. Otra Dr.
Ivans, UT 84738
Phone: (435) 673–5458
Custom copper metal work

Eron Johnson Antiques, Ltd.
451 Broadway
Denver, CO 80203
Phone: (303) 777–8700
Fax: (303) 777–8787
www.eronjohnsonantiques.com
Lighting and colonial furnishings

Gallery 24
Karen Kesler
Sally Elliot
P.O. Box 750368
Torrey, UT 84775
Phone: (435) 425–2124
www.gallery24.biz
Folk art, pottery, paintings, and artistic furniture

Michael Haskell Antiques
539 San Ysidro Rd.
Montecito, CA 92108
Phone: (805) 565–1121
Fax: (805) 565–1541
www.michaelhaskell.com
Seventeenth- and eighteenth-century Spanish Colonial antiques

Lizard Breath Ranch Designs
Janey Katz
HC 75 Box 81
Galisteo, NM 87540
Phone: (505) 466–1966
www.lizardbreathranch.com
Whimsical metal sculptures from old cars

Mediterrania
15770 N. Greenway
Scottsdale, AZ 85260
Phone: (480) 991–2646
Country antiques and furnishings

Morning Star Traders
2000 E. Speedway Blvd.
Tucson, AZ 85719
Phone: (520) 881–3060
www.morningstartraders.com
Mexican Colonial home furnishings

Old Hickory Furniture Co.
Craig Campbell
403 S. Nobles St.
Shelbyville, IN 46176
Phone: (800) 232–2275
www.oldhickory.com
Natural hickory furniture

Olsen Wrought Iron
1250 W. Sunset Blvd. A3
St. George, UT 84770
Phone: (435) 674–5354
Fax: (435) 656–5677
Custom wrought iron

Opuzen Hand Painted Fabrics
Felicia
5794 Venice Blvd.
Los Angeles, CA 90019
Phone: (323) 549–3489
Fax: (323) 549–3494
Hand painted fabrics

Osborn Labor Temple
Kevin Osborn
167 S. Stone
Tucson, AZ 85701
Phone: (520) 624–2756
Pottery

Ottoman Treasures
P.O. Box 441
801 S. Highland St.
Mt. Dora, FL 32757
www.ottomantreasures.com
Phone: (352) 383–6286
Fax: (352) 383–6317
Old-world artifacts, specializing in items from Turkey

R. Furniture by Olinda Romani
7219 Alabama Ave.
Canoga Park, CA 91303
Phone: (818) 592–0815
Fax: (818) 592–0846
www.rfurniture.com
Handmade colonial furniture

Dramatic cloud formations are common in the desert. Cliffs formed by wind and water are rich in iron, making the soil red. In this painting, fine artist Kim Whitesides masterfully captures the drama of the desert on canvas.

PHOTO BY KIM WHITESIDES

Carved, constructed, and
upholstered by a fine
craftsman, this original
lounge is inviting to the
eye as well as the body.
Shown at Gallery 24 in
Torrey, Utah.

Raymisa
Walter Paredes
Juan Moore 199
P.O. Box 4208
Lima 100, Peru
Phone: (051–I) 446–6951
www.raymisa.com

Rhodes, Ragen & Smith
Raymond Whelan
409 Wall St.
Ketchum, ID 83340
Phone: (208) 725–5233
Fax: (208) 725–5233
Antique and handcrafted building products

Rustic Stuff
Paul Faulk
16815 N. 67th Place
Phoenix, AZ 85254
Phone: (602) 617–9781
e-mail: rustic-stuff@cox.net
Furniture designer, interior designer

S. Gallery
Sherry Thompson
Tower at Ancestor Square
2 West St. George Blvd.
St. George, UT 84770
Phone: (435) 688–0451
*Custom furniture, updated southwestern
art and accessories*

Silver Plume
Cheryl Jackson
800 S. E. Hawthorn
Portland, OR 97214
Phone: (503) 235–8328
Original rustic furniture and accessories

PHOTO BY MARY WHITESIDES

Stratford Court
Antiques & Interiors
Scottsdale Fashion Square
4848 E. Cactus
Scottsdale, AZ 85254
Phone: (480) 990–1092
Spanish Colonial antiques, reproductions, and accessories

Touch of History
David Farca
15507 N. Scottsdale Rd. #160
Scottsdale, AZ 85254
Phone: (480) 991–8898
www.touchofhistory.com
Old-world Spanish Colonial furniture

Tribal Links
Phyllis Woods
167 S. Stone Studio F
Tucson, AZ 85701
Phone: (520) 623–8654
Recycled glass chandeliers and African artifacts

Virgin River Rustics
Mike Crawford
P.O. Box 790237
St. George, UT 84779
Phone: (435) 635–3362
Fax: (435) 635–7126
Furniture craftsman

Kim Whitesides, Artist
926 E. Sage Park Lane
Salt Lake City, UT 84117
Phone: (801) 268–3090
Old-world still life, southwestern landscape

INTERIOR DESIGNERS

2 Design
Chris Evans
2 West St. George Blvd.
St. George, UT 84770
Phone: (435) 673–9796
Interior design, old-world Tuscany style

Paula Berg Design Associates Inc.
7522 E. McDonald
Scottsdale, AZ 85251
Phone: (480) 998–2344
Fax: (480) 951–0165

Casa Fina Interior Design
Michael Rennick
2307 Santa Clara Dr. #20
Santa Clara, UT 84765
Phone: (435) 656–1677
Interior design, old-world Tuscany style

Denton House Interiors
Joey Butchen
52 Exchange Place
Salt Lake City, UT 84102
Interior design

Jill Jones
2410 W. Entrada Trail #48
St. George, UT 84770
Phone: (435) 688–1080
Fax: (435) 688–1042
Updated southwestern style

Rustic Stuff
Paul Faulk
16815 N. 67th Place
Scottsdale, AZ 85254
Phone: (602) 617–9781
Furniture designer, interior designer

Jo Taulbee
7904 E. Chaparral #456
Scottsdale, AZ 85250
Phone: (480) 595–1896; (800) 950–5512
Old-world interiors

Vision Design Group, Inc.
David Naylor
1807 Second St. #2
Santa Fe, NM 87505
Phone: (505) 988–3170
Fax: (505) 982–7592
Old-world interiors, updated southwestern

MATERIALS AND FINISHES

Ardex Engineered Concrete
400 Ardex Park Dr.
Aliquippa, PA 15001
Phone: (724) 203–5000
Fax: (724) 203–5001

The Blue Book of Building and Construction
www.thebluebook.com

Decorative Iron
10600 Telephone Rd.
Houseton, TX 77075
Phone: (888) 380–9278
Fax: (713) 991–6493
www.decorativeiron.com
sales@decorativeiron.com

Georgia O'Keefe is famous for her walks in the desert. She always brought found objects home with her that became the inspiration for many of her paintings. The harsh sun and desert conditions have a way of honing and polishing bones into works of art in and of themselves. Here steer skulls define desert style on a porch.

PHOTO BY MARY WHITESIDES

Federal Supply Source
Phone: (800) 352–2852
Lists of water-saving supplies

Jefferson Recycled Woodworks
1104 Firenze Rd.
Box 696
McCloud, CA 96057
Phone: (530) 964–2740
Goodwood@snowcrest.net

Pinecrest Doors
2118 Blaisdell Ave.
Minneapolis, MN 55404–2490
Phone: (800) 443–5357
Fax: (612) 871–8956

School of Italian Plasters
Phone: (866) 560–4444

Sweets Catalog for Building Materials
www.sweets.construction.com

Tiamca Venetian Plaster
8828 South Hardy Dr.
Tempe, AZ 85284
Phone: (480) 783–0676
Fax: (480) 932–8230

Venetian Plaster Finishes
Phone: 44 (0) 28–2954–0601
www.classicwalls.com
infor@classicwalls.com

Water Saving Toilets
Sanitary for All
3909 Wilmer Rd.
Niagara Falls, NY 14305
Phone: (800) 363–5874
Fax: (519) 824–1143

WILDFLOWER HOTLINES

Desert Botanical Garden
Phoenix, AZ
Phone: (480) 481–8134
Hotline: (480) 941–1225

Peralta Trail
Superstition Wilderness
Mesa, AZ
Phone: (800) 354–4595

Picacho Peak State Park
Tucson, AZ
Phone: (520) 466–3183

Tucson Botanical Gardens
Tucson, AZ
Phone: (520) 325–9255

U.S. Forest Service
National Hotline
Phone: (800) 354–4595

White Sands National Monument
Southern New Mexico
Phone: (505) 679–2599, ext. 236 or 223

Bibliography

Bowers, Janice Emily. *Shrubs and Trees of the Southwest Deserts.*
Western National Parks Assoc., 1994.

Brenzel, Kathleen Norris, ed. *Sunset Western Garden Book*, Rev. ed.
Menlo Park, California: Sunset Books, 2001.

Epple, Anne Orth & Lewis E. *A Field Guide to Plants of Arizona,*
5th ed. Helena, Montana: Falcon Publishing, 1997.

Houk, Rose and Huey, George H. *Wild Cactus.* New York:
Artisan, 1996.

Mail Order Catalog. *Plants of the Southwest.* Santa Fe, New
Mexico.

Perl, Philip. *Cacti and Succulents: An Encyclopedia of Gardening Series.*
New York: Time Life Books, 1978.

Salman, David. *A High Country Garden.* Santa Fe, New Mexico:
Fall Catalog, 1995.

Williamson, Darcy. *Wild Foods of the Desert.* Bend Oregon:
Maverick Publications, 1985.

WEBSITES

Classic Wall Finishes, www.classicwalls.com

Coachella Valley Water District, www.cvwd.or

Desert Botanical Garden of Phoenix, www.dbg.org

Desert USA, www.desertusa.com

Earth Work, www.architecturemag.com

Environmental Marketing Group, www.newvillage.com

The Living Desert, www.livingdesert.org

Penn State College of Engineering, www.engr.psu.edu

Southwestern New Mexico online,
http://southernewmexico.com

Photography Credits

Erika Blumenfeld
xii, 5–7, 111–13, 116, 126

Lydia Cutter
x, 111

Karen Kessler
93

Katsuhisa Kida
vi–vii, 88—92, 94–95, 128–29

Gayle Pepper
99

Jessie Whitesides
115

Kim Whitesides
122

Mary Whitesides
1—6, 13, 21, 29, 34, 42, 61–62, 65, 96–97, 100, 102–3,
105–6, 109, 114, 117, 123–24